LOSGET
PRESS

First edition
Zen U Poems 1

Poems by Zen U
Illustration by Zen U
Translated by Nilicon Bones
Edited by Nilicon Bones
Author Photography by Nilicon Bones
Design and Layout by Nilicon Bones

Losget Press
2025

Zen U, Qingdao, China, 1990s.
Photo by Nilicon Bones.

This English collection gathers eight long poems by the genius poet Zen U, selected from her poetry series "Some People" and translated from the original Chinese by Nilicon Bones. Her poems never seek deliberate polish; instead, they let the flood-like primal force from deep within surge forth. This force is enough to shatter words and present intense reality truthfully.

III

LOSGET
Published in the United States by Losget Press,
Los Angeles.
Originally published in paperback in the United
States by Losget Press in 2025.
Names: U, Zen, author.
Title: Zen U Poems 1
Description: First edition. | Los Angeles: Losget
Press, 2025.
ISBN: 978-1-951364-47-2
Subjects (LCSH): Human condition—Poetry |
Identity (Psychology)—Poetry | Memory—Po-
etry | Body, Human—Poetry | Survival—Poetry
| Food—Poetry | Factories—Poetry | Fathers—
Poetry | Los Angeles (Calif.)—Poetry | Paradise
(Calif.)—Poetry | Chinese poetry—21st centu-
ry—Translations into English
Classification: LCC PL2947.U46 E5 2025 (print)
| DDC 895.116—dc23
Book design by Nilicon Bones.
First printed in the United States in 2025.
E-mail: losgetpress@gmail.com

Contents

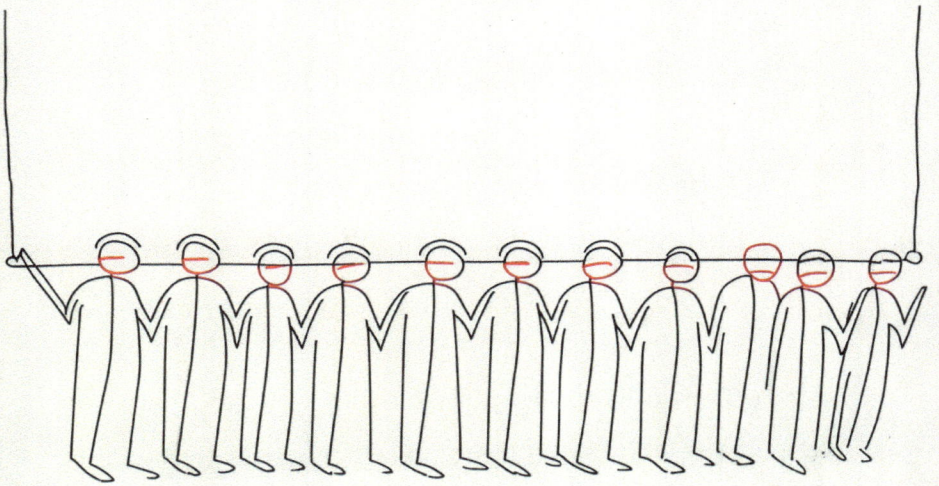

A Person

The new baby
lies in the center of the bed,
born at the most auspicious hour.
People who are about to disperse
surround him with grand gift boxes,
golden plates, saying
blessings.
They pile up into a huge thing
that will one day weigh upon
the baby's road ahead.

I have limbs, unused.
I have a face
with no expressions yet.
He — doesn't yet know how to perform.
We know.
They know.

Look – you all have known all along.

They're all laughing.

Come, little one, laugh like us.

I – don't know what that is.

A child – stands

in the center of the ground.

The others all possess

white sneakers, red ribbons,

running in circles,

praising greatness.

Only I am barefoot,

quietly crying.

Tomorrow you enter this gate once more –

therefore, you must join our ranks, celebrate.

Be joyful as we are,

whether you – have shoes and ribbons or not,

open your mouth, swallow your tears.

Sadness is forbidden.

I have clothes and hats.
I have cigarettes
and alcohol.
I have sterile black gloves.
But they all — wear white gloves,
waving,
with the sun behind them
that never sets.
Longevity plastic flowers
are growing underfoot.

Come on — this is the best age.
Shout loudly with us:
Life is so good!

A young man
stands in the center of the ground.
In the distance,
the last train has just stitched up the night.
Nearby, sleepless people
stir up yellow dust.

Come on, kid, laugh with us.
Why do I need to know what that is?
Look – you surely know.
You've known for a long time.
Even the fiercest lions
have learned to grin for food.

And he
is like a piece of wood
by the wall, stripped of leaves.
Those beasts all bear three scars.
And I – bear seven.

This is the playbill.
The strings are strong, ready for use.
We'll tie up your limbs
and your facial features.
At the moment of climax,
you won't see anything –
but we will.

Here, once again,
a new comedy character
will be born.

Come look – look:
This old man in black clothes,
with white hair, is laughing.
All the proper people
in white clothes,
lifting the long coffin,
sending off the gray ancestors.

Even the sky couldn't help
shedding heavy rain.
And he's still here,
still laughing.

So let it be, old man.
Come join us – just cry.
Isn't it good
to be one of the mourners

at such a sorrowful time?

The old man
stands in the middle of the road.
They've long forgotten
to unhook the strings that control
my upturned smile.
They have sunk into my bones.

Look – this madman.
Right this moment,
he's laughing – like crying.
What a fool.

Come on – follow us.
Crying is what's right.
You don't belong.

The folded baby
lies in the center of the bed.
I have no clothes yet.

All the people surround him.
And you
know no one there.

Countless silhouettes
swarm like storm clouds,
blanketing the sky.
The pink baby turns ashen gray.

I, as the first ancestor,
am weeping.
Just begin to speak
in a lost, primordial tongue.
The calculating people
all laugh.

Tonight,
I – am still not
a person.

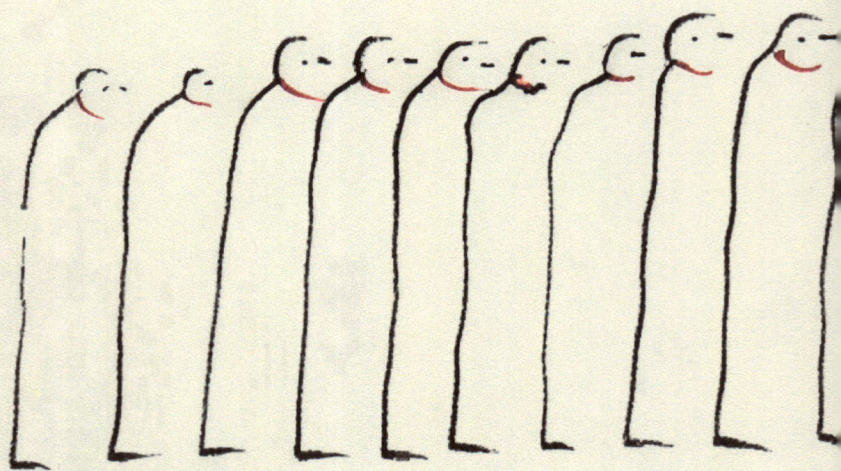

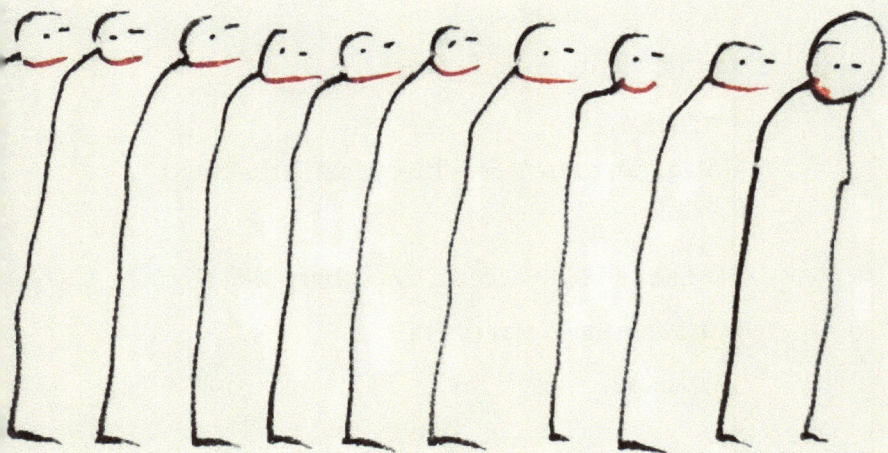

Estate Sale

That man
runs back and forth, again and again,
on Clover Street, looking
for a lucky four-leaf clover.
Hey, hey,
up ahead, there's free breakfast, breakfast.

He uses a blues accent, eyes sharp like a spirit,
announcing to strangers
the gospel.

Here, the short trees with red flowers
lean against the half-height houses.
Here, the pets never leave home.
The hot wind of three seasons
blows everything away,
even shadows can't stay.

Only for a moment before dawn,

gospel songs pass through here.

Hey, you, you, up ahead,

there's free breakfast, breakfast, breakfast.

That man,

that voice, on that day,

stopped abruptly.

At that time, four-leaf clovers bloomed all along the roadside.

But he went somewhere unseen, searching.

L.A.'s blazing sun can't burn him anymore.

Maybe on Clover Street there,

free breakfast waits, and also

free lunch and dinner.

Today, Clover Street is bustling.

People of all colors

come looking for four-leaf clover luck.

In a Mississippi-style room,

there's real free breakfast and all the belongings.

People who are full leave content,

everyone getting something.

Flies move in and out calmly,
searching for scraps, passing through shadows
standing in the corners of walls.
Hey, you all, you've taken all the four-leaf clovers,
and the free breakfast, breakfast, breakfast.
The sneakers under the porch are covered in dust.
Bones in the dark room
are blue, shining with a starlike gleam.
Hey, you, sorry, this place is already empty.

That man
must have gotten the free breakfast
up ahead, far away, and everywhere,
and the lucky four-leaf clover.
Strangers simply took away
all he had gathered.
The room where he once lived is waiting
to be filled with a new owner.

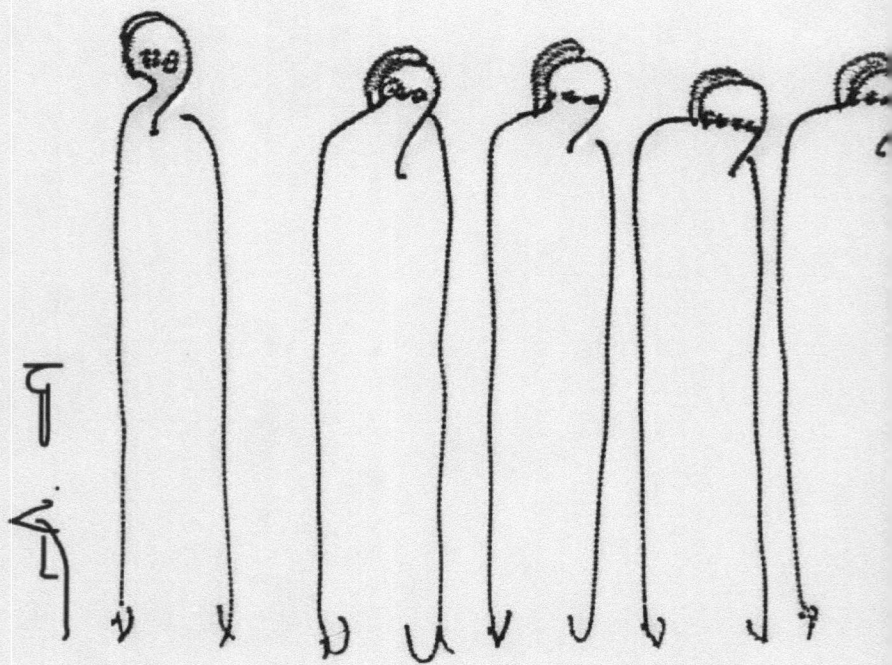

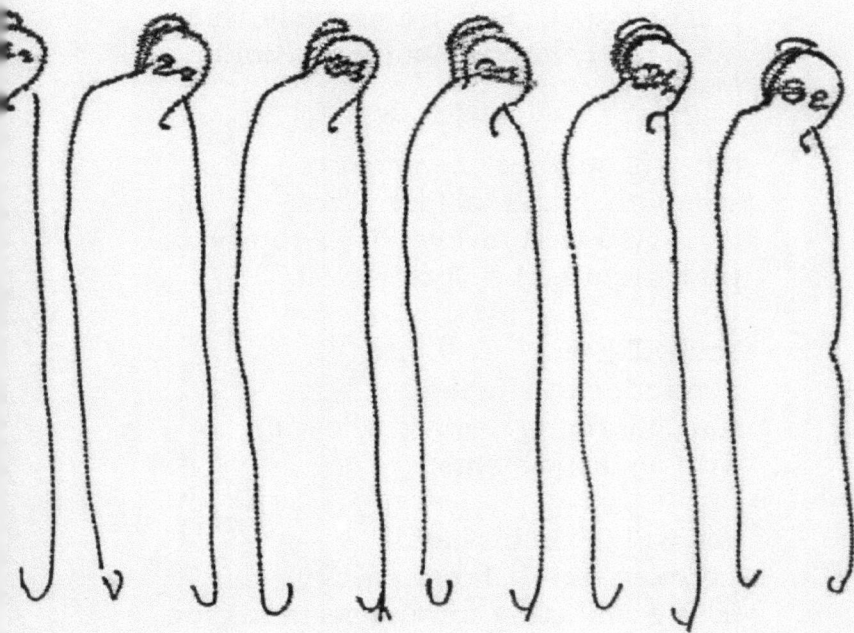

2

You will see
that painting,
see that person,
still on paper, cloth, frame, table, wall,
desperately hiding something, holding it in
his arms.

You will only see one person:
a smooth, maternal face gazes
through uncertain eyes like a rotary dial,
yet certain as they look at you.

You will hear
him suddenly singing,
startled, angry, sorrowful, joyful,
with no instruments.

You will see in his hand
a broken record, far too heavy,
falling while tiny sprouts begin to grow,
and four fingers strive hard to rescue.
Inside the spider-like belly,
once filled with red silk threads,
now emptied.

Thin, conservative legs pressed together
on a chair without support, evading motion.

You will hear
him whisper nightly,
confessing to God
in murmurs deep as a whirlpool.

If you borrow tears from an innocent cow,
sorrow will be injected back into his eyes,
and you can firmly gaze at him
when his guard is down.

With new vision, you will learn
to count heads like they do,
count musical notes,
and even more complex fodder.

Then you will discover these are two people,
fused tightly together, as thin as a single form,
hidden in the quietest corner of the world,
inside the painting.

Suddenly enlightened, you will
delete mercy from cow eyes,
draw the matador's sword,
and fiercely tear apart this seamless union.

The child disguised as a record
will be severed, ripped away.

He emits the music box's final ding-dong,
but does not weep.
Only wide, curved plow marks remain on the
painting – those are
his claw marks from crawling and struggling.
He becomes debris, then a tumor,
ultimately, an unnamed, never-existing per-
son.

Spotlights in the gallery keep chasing and
biting tightly
the one who hid the child.
Now he truly remains alone.

Confession's heat has cooked him thoroughly;
his broken protection leaves him utterly de-
feated.
At this moment,
you no longer need to use the cow's tears,
and he will hide no more.
The dead child slowly slips from his embrace,
accumulating like snowflakes, melting away.

On the wall, only nails remain.
Neither human nor bovine tears can ever wit-
ness anything again.

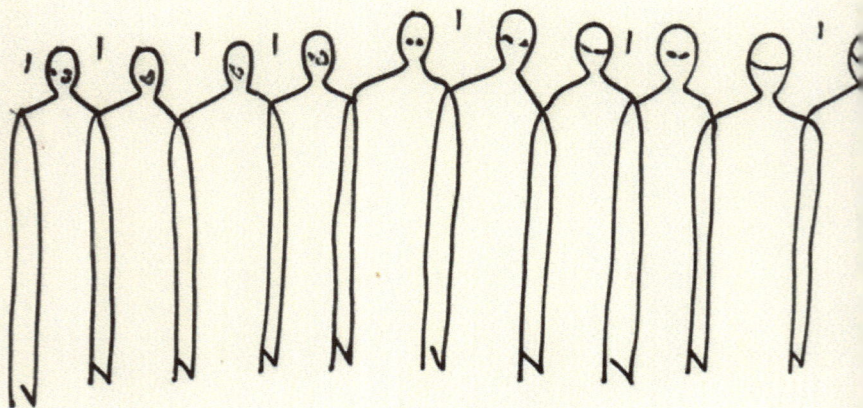

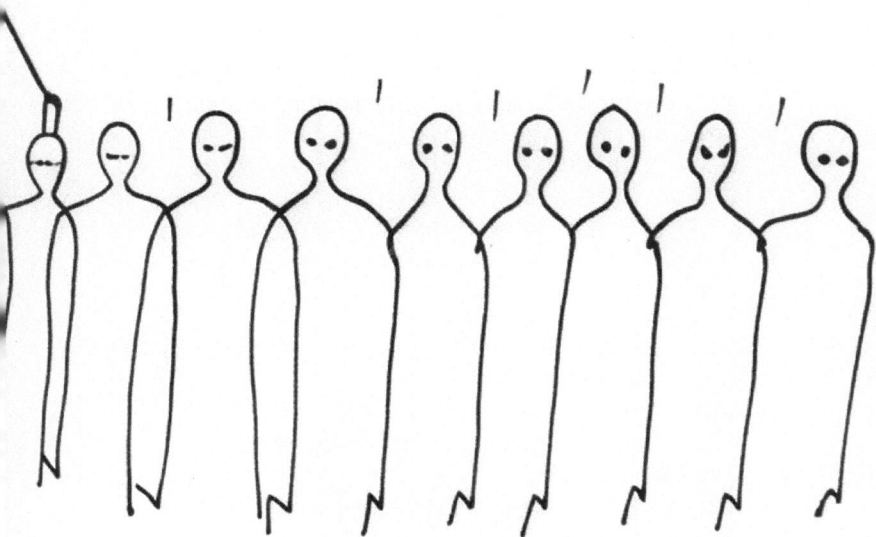

The One Unable to Grieve,
Captivated by Grief

Mm, Ma,
I still remember the woman on your dress,
a serpent's tail behind her, under yellow moon-
light,
staring at me with hollow eyes, signaling
mystery, prophecy:
Someone will have ten years left, no longer
than a wanderer's song.
Back then, we did not care.

Your backpack is always filled with fruit hard
candy scent.
Clear cellophane rustles,
tempting shameless saliva, tongues.
Mm, Ma,
You love talking yet seldom speak.
Inability is the name you carry
in another surname's genealogy.

If we run north in the coldest winter,
white wind over the salt flats
Snatches the iron cup we hold tight,
spilling last night's saved lunch.
We must chase the lid beheaded by wind
until it stops rolling a thousand steps away.
Inside Department Store No. 6, a race has already
begun —
to see who can sell faster.

The seven thirty bell keeps ringing until
varicose-veined bodies obey and take their places.
Mm, Ma, you work the abacus well,
counting tangled accounts with misshapen fingers.

At noon, hot soup gulp gulped down,
loosens frozen, clotted intestines.
Across the counter,
idle people poke the iron stove all year, tongues
busy.
In winter, the most fashionable scent
is simply scorched steamed bread.
Frozen cabbage stews,
melting small, floating bits of pork fat.
Yet we must stay alert:
Aluminum lunch boxes stand in boiling combat;
Should they lose, lunch will be seized and swal-
lowed by spiteful coal cinders.
Only the oft lost lid left behind.
Mm, Ma,
You must be careful, again and again,
Or we'll lose the meal.

You have a girl who cries easily –
Everyone knows.
At the annoying age, she tries to exhaust
a lifetime of tears;
In the future she will be dried out.
Lions were born in August.
Someone – already smelling blood,
someone's nose, blocked by fate, now reeks.
We all see – the tenth year –
his swelling rage still prospers –
even with a giant body, it cannot contain
the prophecy about to burst.

He divides the food among us – stingy, yet trying
to be fair.
He hangs the leftover scraps of meat high to keep
them from thieves,
leaving a few floating pieces of unsettled emotion
to drift all around.

Mm, Dad,
The factory in Beiling was once red – in the vast
expanse, the Sifang,
buried under rusted nails for many years.
At night the thin guard dog will see the city's weak
lights,
holding back the hidden fear; there,
workers drag long shadows, mumbling to the ma-
chines
overtime – never ending.
They turn out sharp-edged sorrow that fills the
warehouse.

Don't eat yet – you all, wait.
I'll bring back steamed buns tasting of machine
oil,
in a dented aluminum lunch box,
along with hot fried fish and eggplant. Wait.
Mm, Dad,
Back then our wine was scarce;
There was no need to tell real from fake.
On the wall the handed down cracked clock keeps
clanging –
It warns, over and over,
that its brown descendant will be mortgaged to
lies.
Time – at night tries to stop, but lies awake.
No one knows – the battery is just for show; wind-
ing is how it runs.

Maybe if it stopped, it wouldn't consume
what life is left. Mm, Dad,
You – may already know, while we still know
nothing.

Every day, you strain to make out
the smeared digits on a grimy, worn out telephone
dial, redialing again and again,
trying to reach the child who went far away,
and I, forever on the looping stairwell,
run up and down until exhausted,
yet you remain unfound.
Mm, Dad, you won't know:
My ear has lost the handset; the line will never
connect;
nor can I see where you – keep dialing the wrong
number.
And we all remain unfound,
unable to reach
the real exit, the actual place, or the honest words.

Mm, Dad,
Inside your black faux leather bag, printed with
the white Zhanqiao Pier,
there is always a glowing red coal mine,
trying to warm – whoever is the next one losing
heat.
You have to ride the foot brake bicycle to look for
it.
The mute hint from the woman with a serpent tail
– no one ever believes it,
Yet in the dark green night you hear the sound of
superstition growing old.
You have to drop the bag in panic and run,
Then pick it up again for courage.
Mm, Dad,

That really can keep our 36.8 degrees for a while,
But it can't hold your own warmth.

Why were you, in the south facing room on Xin-
glong Road,
undone by a cup of wine and a bowl of tofu?
Even when the whole place counted down, you
never rose again – what a riddle.
There was no cheering then, only wailing.
Mm, Dad,
Is that a loss or a win?
The woman who held you was not the one with the
serpent tail.
On her grieving arm your five red fingerprints still
remain.
In the future the inept her
still refuses to live with you – far away,
the woman of shared blood who offered her last
grain for you
weeps day and night.
In the future she will lose all her kin as well.
And I can only stay silent, out of sight of anyone.

Polished stainless steel display stands
set out forty nine former YOUs in neat rows.
None can come back like immortal cats,
can't go stand behind the grimy freight yard,
counting every season to come.
Do you remember the dog lying in shadow? – It
still needs leftovers.
Sometimes it talks; its eyes already blank.
Mm, Dad,
Didn't you have a voice that shook the earth –
shining from birth?
An ancestor once said:
A demi-immortal child always skilled at flipping

everything,
so please proclaim ascent – eternal life – but
the reversal was blocked by 401's iron door –
now marked 404.

You'll no longer see white sorrow; your hair is still
black.
The last life you let go
is methodically placed into a dark red box, a tiny
image,
fixed in an oval vintage frame,
with all colors faded away to convey solemnity.

Mm, Mom,
He has seen – he can see:
You, aging woman, daily, faithfully burning in-
cense,
trying again and again to summon your soul with
toothbrush and paste.
She speaks home words, lays out plain dishes,
offering them with reverence –
Until one day in the west,
six pairs of footprints depart into the distance,
back turned – telling her in her dream he will not
return.

I saw no scene then;
I was up north, hating someone who'd betrayed
me.
Home was too far for laughter or tears to flow
back.
A sliver of dawn light pierced thick walls,
insisting on touching you, fourteen turns away.
Mm, Dad,
so silent – you who once roamed everywhere –
have pure furnace flames burned you clean? They

say:
one who sees the unseen once saw
a sluggish, blurred figure
dragging steps worn through the soles,
reverently visiting the stern grandmother once
more,
then closing the old door softly and walking off.

Back then the neighbor's old cat was seeing
through history,
It wouldn't notice your arrival.
You still miss the freshly baked bun –
it might store a few hours of energy
but can't sustain you on the long round trip. So,
you, like me, can no longer return.
Mm, Dad, home is too far –
our home was too far. That day:
the ones best at mending people gave up.
They wore ominous white robes – not the wedding
kind.
No one dares wrestle with fate, especially on
nights of lightning and thunder.

Mm, Dad,
I'm here – I'm back.
Please lie down – before the dark red foam over-
flows.
May I use the ancient bloodletting method again –
for one last try?
Hands, legs,
Arms,
Chest,
the stiff, slack belly, the taut, dark purple face.
I have tried every wound with sharp regret.
Every cut reveals emptiness, and you feel nothing.
I'm sorry, so sorry,

please don't hurry down this uneasy night road,
Dad,
or the black shadow will erase you.
Please stop, just stop –
May I try – the final method:
using death to heal death?

We've changed into white mourning clothes and
donned black armbands.
Words and tears lose their direction; we won't
know –
you're racing desperately on a reversed route.
The road name leads to the old home,
yet the direction has been turned by the wind.
You keep racing home with all your might.
Yet you go farther and farther away.

Mm, Dad,
Please sit – like a god – and rest,
place your useless head at your feet, and forget
everything.
You have no right to grieve.
Yes, he cannot grieve.
She gradually forgets sorrow.
And I – am captivated by grief.

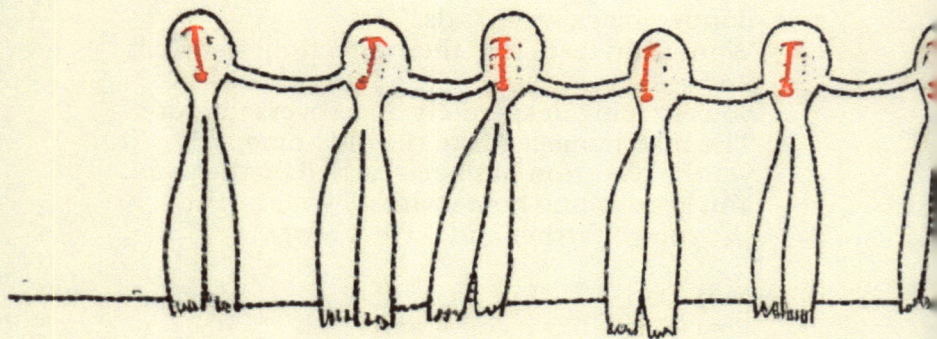

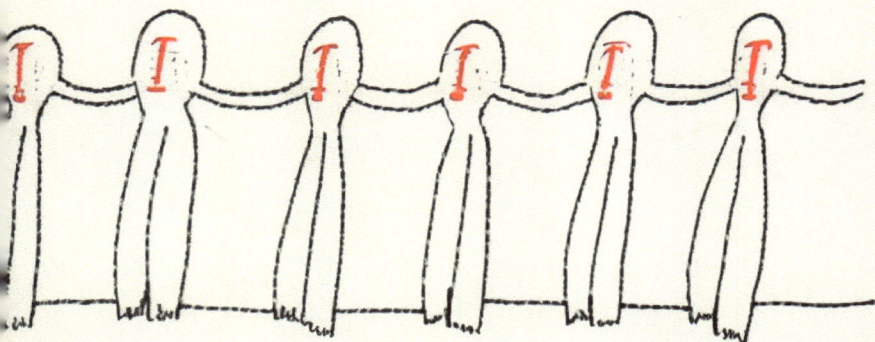

Mana

Today's count —
YOUr count today —
the count you could finish TOday, the count you have
finished —
TELL me THE PRECISE NUMBER.

Mana GET AWAY
A bountiful soul fit for pressing oil — someone
has already begun SOLO beats for tally:
cling-clang, cling-clang, cling-clang.

Forbidden rose gloves — forbidden!
All gloves — let thorns grow from fingers
to match the speed of blood.
Cling-clang, cling-clang.

November rain falls without stop — ding-dong, ding-
dong.
Forget your body, forget your damp self.
No sofa, no bed here, and no lazy stool.
If you can't earn the machine's favor,
you won't deserve to hear the pre-lunch bell — ding.

Hurry — speed up!

Let your chamber drive like a piston to avoid rust — a
sound body —
you — will have balance, you will have balance,
able to plant a person,
feed and water it — each day.

Don't stop — cannot stop — YOU — you —
round and round, diligently,
turn those wear-prone knees.
Yet here — no lubrication fits the model.

Look — on the blindfold, the instruction: accelerate,
accelerate.
In two weeks, small silver numbers will arrive.
Mana GET AWAY
Mana GET BACK

Listen:
The squealing millstone is destiny — an aging infant
just found its resting place in your ear, whispering
a tear can never flow between two great souls — spirits
—
gush-gush.

Mana GET BACK
If exhaustion drives you mad, tear off the blindfold
and free your eyes,
you'll see the millstone spilling crimson life, and
the grand ideals in its grinding already pulped.

Mana GET AWAY — swish-swish!
Roll, roll far away,
far into the age of the old god
where they were starving in the wilderness.

Mana suddenly falls from the sky —
white, fragrant towers rise from bare earth — ah, ah!
Mana, Mana — they never stop eating.
The stuffed bellied bosses reap down miracles,
belching clinking golden burps — belch, belch.

Mana GET BACK
The human form is a bottomless pit;
no new god or old god can fill it —
gurgle, gurgle.

Hunger will chase the feeding bowl — quick — go!
Offer your fleece and sacrifice — baa, baa, baa, baa.
Mana always lies ahead.
Hollow bellied workers must learn to mind their
rations.

MONEY MONEY
Mana Mana
Blindfold your eyes and follow the machine,
and Mana will fall from the sky — Mana na na.

Follow the bosses' rhythm:
one, two, three, four, five, six — complete
your tally,

and it will carry you forth to the Sabbath.

MONEY MONEY — look, look, look —
this is about hunger and balance — that day
you will find — all the Mana there is,
nothing but morning dew.

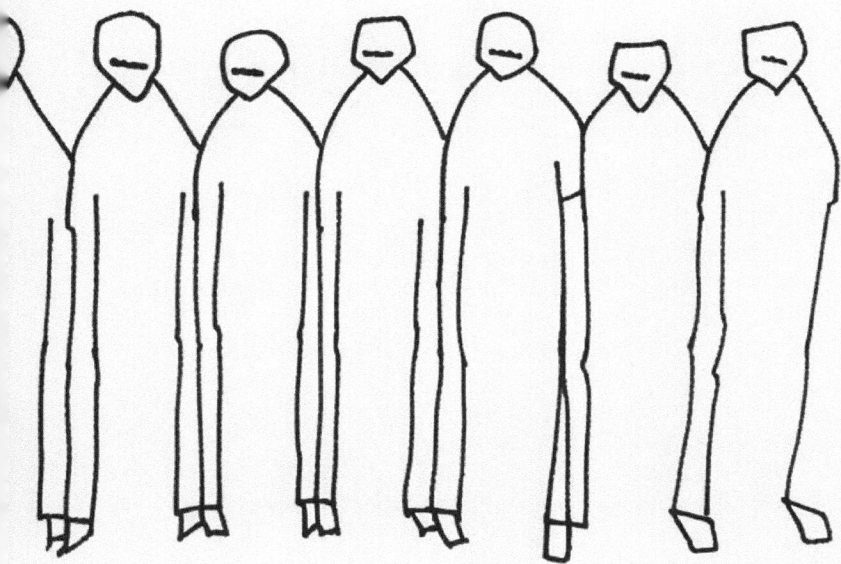

The Drifter

I have no way back to my hometown —
can only see my mother's knees mirrored in a cup
of water —
no way to turn, no one to guide me
back along the old road.
I no longer have a hometown. Every road
is sealed by floating locks,
the keys turned to weeds.
When I want to meet my father's skull at night,
I need to get a wine glass,
pour a small glass of cheap rotgut, and drink it
down.
Then I hear a sound, silent as dead ashes.
I see him,
piercingly clear, ever turning,
speaking in a frozen voice, delivering scolding.
If I keep listening
to his sorrow playing from an outdated machine,
over and over,
the nonexistent RAM will gather dust,
neglecting every system.
The more I take in,
the more sorrow and anger I perceive.

Should I sleep?
Can it stop anything?
The hometown in my dreams is untraceable —
there,

the sound of the dark night is sharp and piercing.
The slow witted patient,
always dragging his mother on hasty treks,
bound to treatment year after year.
He has inherited
a violent voice and meticulous, trivial filial piety
still entangled by poor ancestors
perpetuating more useless inheritance.
I have to keep vigil for him, or else
his swollen, festering eye bags
stash precious cheap rotgut
enough to guzzle for eternity.
On scattered nights,
he mumbles his testament,
slurring as he holds back urine.

I cannot stay here,
in any place where the weather, being hot enough
to sear off eczema,
where rumor-bullets are always ready to fire – or
already fired,
where wavering gazes and cowardly sighs
are just enough to aim and channel anger.
So I must maintain
a fixed, pleasant expression as a shield to block.
I am still here.
Here and there – sometimes hard to tell apart.
Between a table and a bed
stand hastily built fortresses.
Whether gaunt or not, I must train diligently
to move lightly, to hide
in a narrow darkness just one square meter wide.
Sorry, people in my hometown.
I cannot see, cannot reach
the spacious rooms where you find rest,
even if they are so close yet out of reach.

Heaven is closed to me –
before death, while living, or even after dying.
Countless lives – sentient or insentient –
still remain inside me, beginning, ending, unable
to be avoided,
digested, dissipated, discarded along the way.
I have never repented.
At first – solemnly – time's armor was put on me.
It was new, then –
Now, dragged down by filth and obscenity, unbear-
ably heavy.
On all my battlefields, I was only resisting myself.
Growth rings interwoven across my body,
clearly inscribed with the history of one defeated.
Offered by devout hands,
kicked back by angels' feet.
Dear God,
I can only bow my head deeply,
avoiding Your holy great light.

I am not going to hell,
whether before death or after.
That place – where only rogues stand.
My experiences are too pure,
every stretch would
be driven out and mocked by the powers of both
sides.
And my faith in the devil
is no greater than in God.
Even if
the merciful gatekeepers there
used the thickest correction fluid,
they could not revise me
a barely passable ticket.
I have to turn back.

Thus, all my life,
I've known to stay clear of will-o'-the-wisps.

I have no way back to the past,
right here in the present. For I
have only one pair of feet – forward yet one-way.
Even in turning, there is only returning
to where the toes were born to face.
Nor am I meant to remain forever in dreams ei-
ther,
even if I force myself to resist sleepiness.
And the old, battle-worn cars, sold off for years,
lie in every unmarked parking lot silently,
waiting to faithfully carry me,
the one who has lost the way of driving,
back.
And I –
am endlessly and anxiously walking on the roads,
searching for them.

I can only –
yet cannot live or not live
in this famous yet unnameable place,
losing all hours,
ignoring gender,
forgetting the left and right of hands,
counting days by the opening and closing of cur-
tains,
killing flies to stay vital,
purifying the entirety
with ancestral cheap rotgut left in my family vat.
If there is a door behind,
strive to lock up the empty gestation,
until it merges with the wall as one.
I –
AM the hometown.

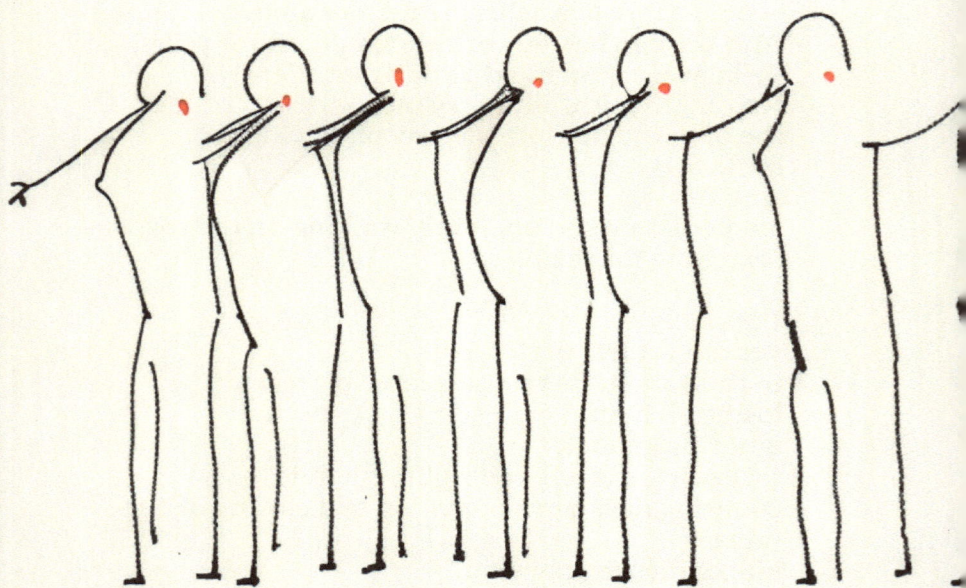

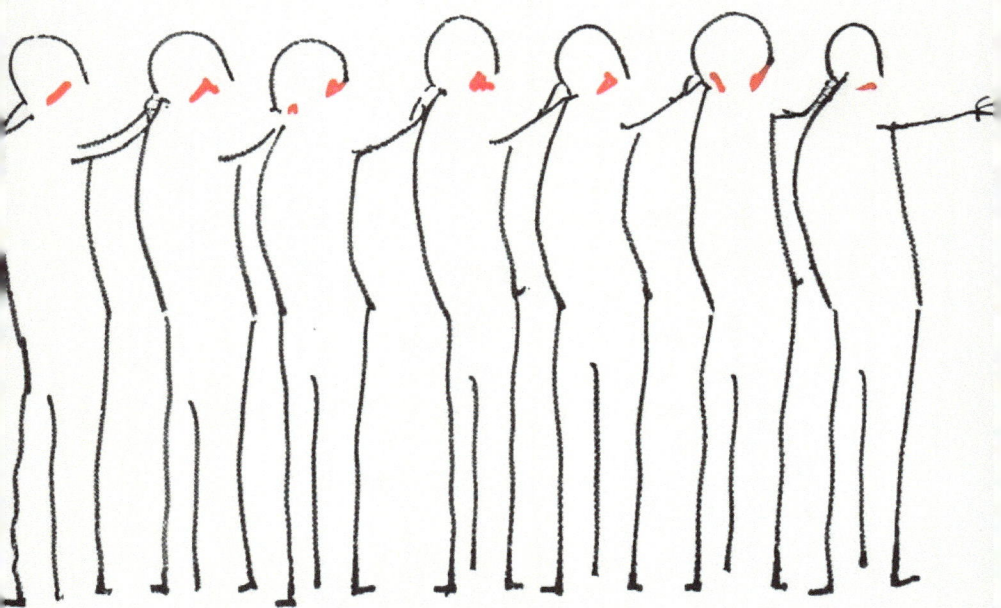

Storage Slot

C4-4-!
Toss in three garments still warm with body heat,
when Paradise woke in shock.
C4-4-?
Already unrecognizable.
Someone riding a blazing red iron steed, trying once
more to part the sea.
Someone — already drowned in the ark of November
2018.

Yet I must go back to search —
C4-4-1.
The Santa Ana wind just swept through Simi Valley —
no one cares
that the cup which once conceived clear water has
withered.
The urge to urinate forcibly shut down.
Stones are busy baking — the scorched earth.

C4-?-1.
There also once were evil thoughts
Growing wildly in the night, endlessly tempting hands
burrowing deep inside, so as
to swiftly seize a little dampness.

Old Faithful once more spouted the dead volcano,
leaving only smoke.
C4-4-1, where are you? Now
it is just a wall.
All colors taken away,
leaving only gray — yet
were those clothes placed
in C4-1-1?
No marks at all.

The base, low platform needs —
to heave up the screen.
Filthy returns always
pretend to be gloomy mountains, sometimes
hiding unexpected five-cent treasures.
Climbers shall veil faces, bow heads
and walk the boundless road.
The hurricane claws the dust raw — it also shrieks in
torment.
Hay entangles the mind; imagination has long since
broken free.

Run, run, go find
C1-1-4.
This is a passage less than ten meters away,
yet the distance is longer than eternity.
In the deep night I cannot go back, cannot turn
around.
Here is Paradise.

Everything must be erased, using all
nonexistent tools.
Only the lucky skeleton faithfully guards the entrance.

C4-4-1, C4-?-1,
C4-4-!, C4-4-?
C3 — already the end.
Where are you?
A drafty roof at Rancho Cucamonga.
Hu Xiuhua, Chen Shuxia — tested LZH3380-LPU-S.
Only names remain, the bags now empty.
By the end of February, snow will fall here.
Even the massive warehouse
shivers in the night. So,
turn off the lights, now stripped of human presence.
Set 1352 — the ever-changing Korean password,
drawing my 37 °C warmth to warm it.

Farewell, you, the one who lost its heat,
the exit is just beyond two doors, where
a faint light flickers all year.
Follow this escape route — run, run,
forget C4, forget
all the storage slots. Remember:
Once you leave, there is no coming back.
In the darkness bereft of homelight glow,
the weapons that once were
solemnly displayed. They
are still waiting for tomorrow's touch.
An empty-cartridge scanner, eyes shut tight,

executes the lingering commands.

Now — the deep night has just begun —
eternal sleep, the most fitting dream.
The pillow has waited too long.
Beep beep, beep beep — again and again.
The password is unlocked — yet
no one shall ever return to C1-4-1.
Even if the cell formatting is reset,
even if every rigid spreadsheet grid is torn open,
even if you run into the barbecue-loving jungle, shed-
ding all clothes —
You will never find the clothes that once were.
The missing inventory must still be somewhere,
must still exist —
in that place where only the name endures.

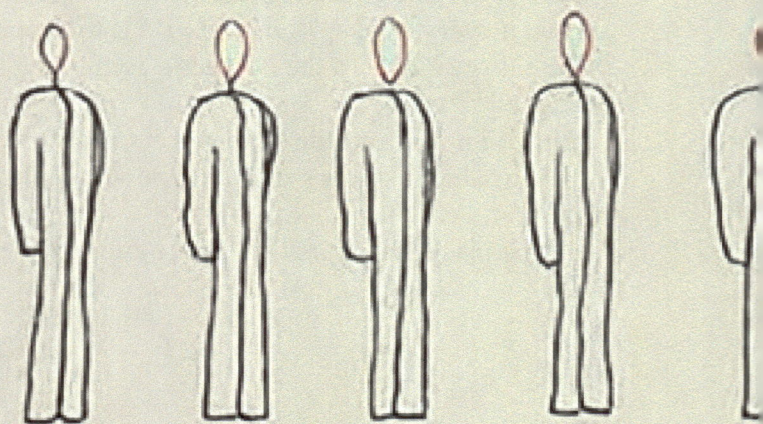

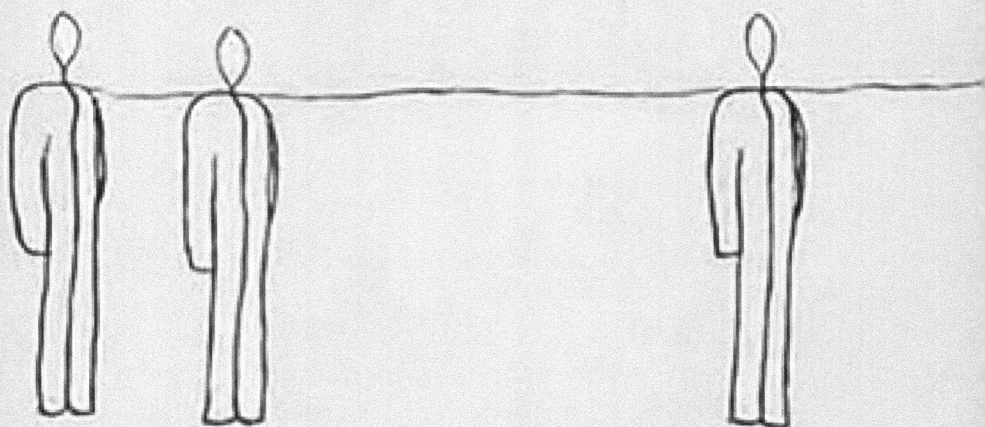

There Are Some

Someone
no longer cares for their hair,
whether long or short, thriving or withered,
seeing it all as wild grass —
left to grow and die on its own.

Someone
never tells their life story
through shallow tattoos;
wrinkles — are the deepest statement.

Someone
need not be written into books,
who fought time repeatedly, defeated repeatedly,
having swallowed — every fallen tooth,
leaving kindness,
to hold up the new shape of the lips.

Someone
with slackened eyelids and blurred expressions,
does not probe into every question —
he knows — there will always be an answer,
one that cannot be given
when the body humbles itself into a question mark.

Someone
has no need to hear,
since youth — has been filling their ear canals,
never distinguishing — strange accents,
leaving only a small, fine shovel — for God.

Someone
never follows
when others move forward. Perhaps,
heading backward, or
at both ends of time,
or even higher, deeper.

Someone
no longer speaks,
having poured out all their words
since the very first cry.

Someone
no longer hesitates,
leaning on a decayed wooden staff, trembling forward.
Nothingness — is the body they cling to,
soon to fall into the depth of reality,
never to climb back.

Someone
no longer swayed by passions.
The sensitive crowds
can no longer keep pace with him.

No one can disturb —
the ever-shortening shadow.

LOSGET

Published in the United States by Losget Press, Los Angeles.
Originally published in paperback in the United States by Losget Press in 2025.
Names: U, Zen, author.
Title: Zen U Poems 1
Description: First edition. | Los Angeles: Losget Press, 2025.
ISBN: 978-1-951364-47-2
Subjects (LCSH): Human condition—Poetry | Identity (Psychology)—Poetry | Memory—Poetry | Body, Human—Poetry | Survival—Poetry | Food—Poetry | Factories—Poetry | Fathers—Poetry | Los Angeles (Calif.)—Poetry | Paradise (Calif.)—Poetry | Chinese poetry—21st century—Translations into English
Classification: LCC PL2947.U46 E5 2025 (print) | DDC 895.116—dc23
Book design by Nilicon Bones.
First printed in the United States in 2025.
E-mail: losgetpress@gmail.com

www.ingramcontent.com/pod-product-compliance
Lightning Source LLC
LaVergne TN
LVHW010034070426
835510LV00006B/127